MINI COLOR SERIES

M2A2 M3A2 Bradley

Backbone of the U.S. Mechanized Infantry

Text by Walter Böhm & Peter Siebert
Illustrations by Hubert Cance

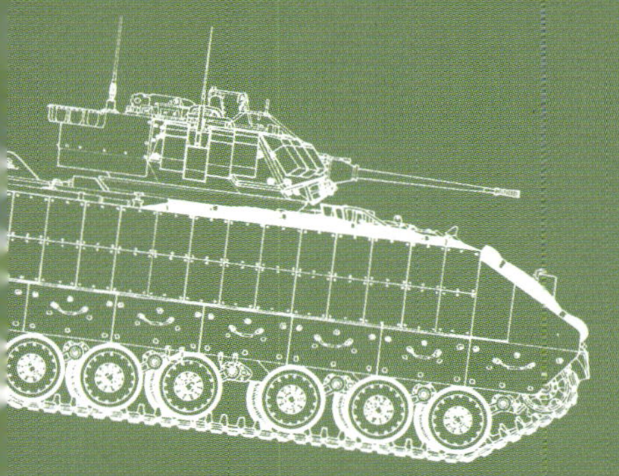

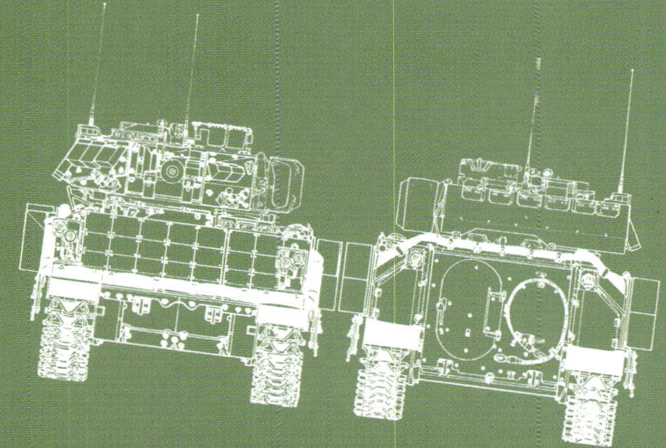

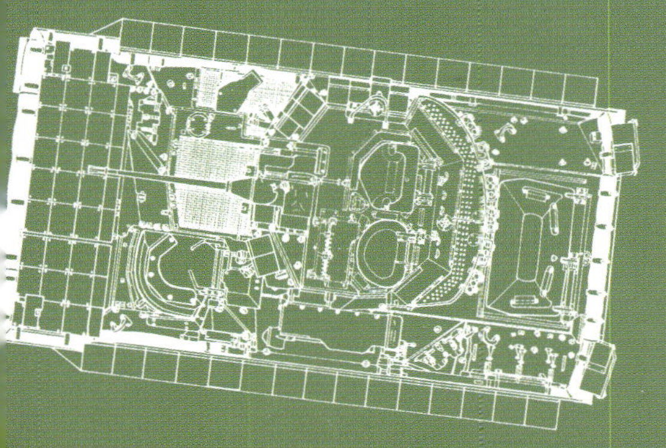

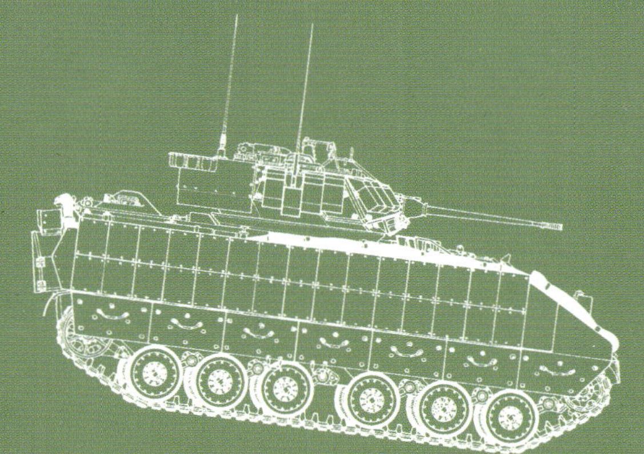

Editor: James R. Hill

by CONCORD PUBLICATIONS CO.
603-609 Castle Peak Road
Kong Nam Industrial Building
10/F, B1, Tsuen Wan
New Territories, Hong Kong
www.concord-publications.com

We welcome authors who can help expand our range of books. If you would like to submit material, please feel free to contact us.

We are always on the look-out for new, unpublished photos for this series. If you have photos or slides or information you feel may be useful to future volumes, please send them to us for possible future publication. Full photo credits will be given upon publication.

ISBN 962-361-671-6
printed in Hong Kong

Glossary

ID: Infantry Division
AD: Armored Division
AR: Armored Regiment
CAV: Cavalry Regiment
INF: Infantry
Mech: Mechanized
Bn: Battalion
Rgt: Regiment
SQDN: Squadron
IFV: Infantry Fighting Vehicle
CFV: Cavalry Fighting Vehicle
MBT: Main Battle Tank
FV: Fighting Vehicle
CMTC Hohenfels:Combat Maneuver Training Center, Hohenfels, Bavaria, Germany
NTC: National Training Center
Stinger: US man-portable ground-to-air missile
TOW: US anti-tank missile
BMP: Soviet infantry fighting vehicle
REFORGER:Return of Forces to Germany, annual USAEUR deployment exercise during the Cold War era
MILES: Multiple Integrated Laser EngagementSystem, using low-power laser projectors and detectors to simulate combat in exercises
MRE: Meal Ready to Eat, US combat ration
MLRS: Multiple Launching Rocket System
FA: Field Artillery
ODS: Operation "Desert Storm", version of Bradley FV
FTX : Field Training Exercise
MICV : Mechanized Infantry Combat Vehicle
ERA : External Reactive Armor
ATGM : Anti-tank Guided Missile

Acknowledgements

Many thanks to the 7th US Army Operation Group Viper for their support, to Ralph Zwilling for some technical information, and to Hartmut Schauer for the foreword.

Picture Credits

Carl Schulze, VS Books, Egon Merk, Greg Stewart, IFOR, and the US Army.

Harmut Schauer

US MECHINF

In 1846, the Regiment of Mounted Riflemen was formed. Two companies mounted on Mexican horses acted as cavalry during the Mexican War, while the rest fought on foot. Half of the Regiment of Voltigeurs and Foot Riflemen was mounted, and each horseman was paired with a foot soldier that was to get up behind him for rapid movement. These two regiments were the first forerunners of modern mechanized infantry, combining mobility with firepower!

In World War I, early tanks offered mobility and some protection to the infantry. During World War II, only the armor division had three armored infantry battalions in half-track personnel carriers. But the post-war armored division was improved with four armored infantry battalions (AIB) and four companies of 208 men each! Beginning in 1948, the M44 fully tracked armored utility vehicle replaced the half-tracks. In 1956, the "Pentomic structure" with five "battle groups" replaced the old regiments. The two armored personnel carrier companies of the divisional transportation battalion were capable of moving an entire infantry battle group. The armored division retained its four armored infantry battalions, the strength increased to 1027 and the units were designated as "armored rifle battalions" (ARB).

The mobility of the armored infantry rifle squad was improved with the help of the M59 armored personnel carrier (APC), a fully tracked amphibious vehicle with ground mobility and agility in water. In 1960, the lighter and less expensive M113 amphibious armored personnel carrier followed. There were seventeen APCs in each armored infantry company and seventy-seven in the armored rifle battalion. The "Reorganization Objective Army Divisions" (ROAD) in 1962 was the real birthday of "mechanized infantry", replacing the armored infantry battalions/armored rifle battalions. The highly mechanized battalions were assigned to armored divisions, standard infantry divisions and new "mechanized infantry divisions" with anti-tank forces. Some mechanized infantry units fought in Vietnam, a "light infantry" war. They used the M113 and M113A1 "battle taxi", which were sometimes employed as fighting vehicles in a tank-like role.

The mechanized 5th Infantry "Bobcats" spent most of their time in Cu Chi trying to stop Viet Cong terrorism and ensure that the roads remained open for safe use by Vietnamese farmers and merchants. Some years after Vietnam, the Infantry School wrote the paper "Mechanized Infantry on the Modern Armored Battlefield", which is an integral and permanent part of the tank-infantry team.

The modern soldier in "mounted warfare" moves quickly under armor protection and dismounts only to fight. To perform their tasks, the infantry asked for a fighting vehicle – more than a carrier – with mobility to keep up with tanks, a stabilized turret and anti-tank capability. The venerable M113 was not the ideal combat vehicle, so the MICV was developed. Finally, in 1983, the US Army received the first Bradley Fighting Vehicles (BFV), a true fighting vehicle. In addition to its greatly increased firepower compared to its predecessor, the M113, the Bradley is also superior in mobility and armor protection. It has a two-man, stabilized turret as a platform for a 25mm Bushmaster chain gun, a 7.62mm M240 coaxial machine gun, and a two-tube TOW launcher with a seven-man dismount team. The 36 Bradley-equipped squads have a "foxhole strength" of 324 fighting soldiers. Operation "Desert Storm" in 1991 was its first crucial test, and it was a complete success.

In the future, the Army Transformation, with its "Objective Force" and "Interim Force", will introduce two new systems: the Light Armored Vehicle (LAV III) as "Interim Armored Vehicle" and the "Mobile Gun System" (MGS). Going back to the roots again: wheels for tracks!

Background - The Threat

In the mid-1980s, at the height of Cold War, weapon technology in the former Soviet Union was progressing. The Soviets were developing more effective ammunition for the main guns of their most modern tanks. As a result, the US Army began a program to give the M2/M3 Bradley better surviability against the threat of the new, upgraded types of Soviet anti-tank ammunition. The focus of a study called "Bradley Block II" was the improved protection for the main components and crew of the M2/M3 Bradley vehicles.

The M2A2 IFV and M3A2 CFV Programs

The main reasons for the development of the A2 Bradley configuration were: upgraded armor protection for the vehicle's hull and turret, modified ammunition stowage, improved back-up sight for the commander, along with a ballistic shield, and internal armor for important components in the interior of the vehicle. As a result of these main modifications, especially the heavier armor, the weight increased to 30 tons. Consequently, the Bradley's drive train and suspension had to be reinforced. Also, the stronger 600hp Cummins VTA-903 engine replaced the former 500hp engine. Since the production of the second "A2" batch in May 1989, all newly produced M2A2/M3A2 Bradleys have been fitted with the new engine. The first batch of 662 vehicles, produced from May 1988 to 1989, still featured the old 500hp engine.

The transmission components, built by General Dynamics Defense System, were also modified to take care of the vehicle's increased weight. Further, the stonger engine made it necessary to upgrade the air cleaners and exhaust system. The newly produced Bradleys in the A2 configuration are fitted with the improved tracks and drive sprocket that have been proven on the MLRS M270 vehicles.

Armament

The M2A2/M3A2 Bradley's main gun is a fully stabilized M242 Bushmaster chain gun. A M240 7.62mm machine gun is mounted coaxial beneath the main gun. A twin-tube TOW 2 anti-tank missile system is mounted in a launcher on the left side of the turret. The TOW 2 system is effective and deadly to all known armor up to ranges of 3000 meters (3280 yards). Two thermal beacons on the box-style TOW launcher allow for tracking and guiding the missiles through all kinds of weather conditions. The system is operable through dust, smoke, rain, and foggy weather, as well as by night.

The night vision equipment of the A2 version includes an AN/PVS-4 day/night thermal vision sight and ISW (Integrated Sight Weapon) fire control system, with optical transfer to the commander's position. The driver is supported by the AN/VVS-2 night vision sight system.

The Hull

The M2A2/M3A2 Bradley's hull is a welded construction, with aluminium No.5083 and 7039. The front and sides are reinforced by armor steelplates. The turret is also welded construction with aluminium No.5083 and reinforced by armor steelplates. The M2A2 IFV (Infantry Fighting Vehicle) has a crew of three – the commander, gunner and driver – and can transport six fully equipped soldiers in the rear. The M3A2 CFV (Cavalry Fighting Vehicle) has the same crew of three, as well as two observers located beneath the rear cargo hatch.

Production

The production line for the M2A2/M3A2 Fighting Vehicles began in the spring of 1988. The first vehicles were delivered to the Army in the autumn of 1988. In 1989/90, the 3rd US INF Division and the 1st US INF Division received their first M2A2/M3A2 Bradleys. By the end of 1994, FMC Corporation had produced a total of 6724 Bradleys, including all updated versions. Threre were 2083 M3s made in the Cavalry Fighting Vehicle configuration and 4641 in the M2 Infantry Fighting Vehicle configuration. The Army plans to upgrade A0 and A1 block Bradleys to the A2 standard. A total of 1423 A2 vehicles should be modified to the A2 ODS (Operation "Desert Storm") level. In the near future, a batch of

1602 Bradley A2s should be upgraded to the common A3 configuration.

Bradley Fighting Vehicles are generally only in service in the US Army. Among foreign countries, only Saudi Arabia has put in an order for M2A2 Bradleys – 400 of them.

Operation Desert Storm - First Fight for the Bradley

The Bradley Fighting Vehicle played a major part in the ground war for the liberation of Kuwait during Operation "Desert Storm". By this time, most USAEUR mechanized infantry battalions and cavalry squadrons were re-equiped from the old M113 to the M2/M3 Bradley, in the versions A0, A1 and A2. From a total of 2200 Bradley vehicles deployed in the desert before the ground war start, 19% were A0 standard, 33% were A1 standard and 48% were the A2 configuration. Just before the war began, some units in the front line received the new A2 vehicles, which were hastily shipped to Saudi Arabia. These tanks came from the POMCUS storage and REFORGER depots in Europe.

In January 1990, the 1-4 CAV of 1st US ID received M3A2s. Most battalions of 1st CAV Division, 1st Armored Division, 2nd Armored Cavalry Regiment and the 3rd Armored Cavalry Regiment had also re-equiped with the A2 standard Bradley. During the fighting in the desert, the brand new M919 25mm ammunition was used. These new rounds, which have a depleted uranium penetrator projectile for the M242 chain gun, were produced only in small numbers and were preferred for use against armored targets. Army statistics show that the gunners of the 1st Armored Division needed only six 25mm rounds to knock out each hostile armored vehicle. This was a result of the excellent gunner training, too.

The main advantages of the Bradley Fighting Vehicle, as shown during "Desert Storm", are high mobility and strong firepower combined with good protection against Iraqi RPGs and anti-tank weapons. The TOW 2 system gives the Bradley an excellent anti-tank capability, and all weapon systems are supported and controlled with the modern thermal sight and night vision systems. During bad weather, at night and in sandstorms, the crews could trust in their sights while the hostile Iraqi crews remained blind in the sand. With their excellent sights, Bradley crews sometimes identified targets earlier than their comrades in M1A1HA Abrams main battle tanks.

During "Desert Storm", the level of reliability of the Bradley fleet was a remarkable 90% readiness. A US Army spokesman reported that only three Bradleys were destroyed by enemy fire, with 17 vehicles being destroyed by friendly fire (mainly from M1A1 120mm guns). The high-survivability improvements of the A2 version were confirmed to be successful during the "Desert Storm" campaign.

The M2A2 ODS/M3A2 ODS Bradley

As a result of Operation "Desert Storm" and the experiences of the troops, an improvement program for the US Army Bradley fleet was begun. These modified vehicles received the code M2A2 ODS/M3A2 ODS (Operation "Desert Storm"). The modifications and update measures included the introduction of a Bradley Eyesafe Laser Range Finder (BELRF), Driver's Vision Enhancer Night Sight (DVE), Digital Compass System (DCS), and a Portable Lightweight GPS Receiver (PLGR) for easier navigation on the battlefield. Yet to be introduced is the Battlefield Combat Identification System (BCIS), which is planned for a later modernization. Today only the M1A1HA Abrams MBT has been updated with the BCIS.

Another future updating for the ODS Bradley will be the AN/VLQ-8 Missile Countermeasure Device (MCD). This system, which should be located on the turret, has the capability to turn away and deceive hostile anti-tank missiles. As a result of the new "3 x 9" mechanized infantry platoon structure, the M2A2 ODS IFV version is fitted with a tenth seat in the rear crew compartment. Also, the driver's position has a new design with a better seat and hatch, and wire cutters are fitted to the hull. In the M3A2 ODS CFV configuration, the seats for the two scouts in the rear were redesigned. For easier handling and maintenance, all ODS Bradley have an electro-hydraulically-operated engine hatch. The hull sides are fitted with eyelets to attach the crew's gear, baggage or water canisters. In 1999, the 1-26 INF and 1-18 INF of the 2nd Dagger Brigade, 1st US ID, who are based in Germany, received their first ODS Bradley M2A2. In August 2000, the M3A2 ODS CFV replaced the M2A2s of 1st Squadron, 4th Cavalry Regiment, 1st US ID, who are based in Schweinfurt, Germany.

Summary

Thanks to the ODS improvement and updating program, the M2/M3 Bradley Fighting Vehicle is still up-to-date and one of the most modern IFV/CFV vehicles in the world. As such, the Bradley will be the backbone of US Army mechanized infantry and cavalry units for the years to come. But military technology is still progressing, so today's US-based units receive brand new M2A3/M3A3-version vehicles.

Variants: Bradley Vehicle System Carrier

When the M2/M3 Bradley fighting vehicle was introduced to the US Army in 1982, a program for a Fighting Vehicle System Carrier based on the Bradley chassis and drive train was begun. The main point was the standardization of vehicle components to simplify and reduce maintenance, logistics and costs. Another reason was the continually ageing M113 versions, which required replacement. A new platform for future weapon systems would be based on Bradley components and parts.

The first weapon system based on the M987 carrier vehicle was the MLRS M270 multiple rocket launcher. During the Gulf War, this artillery system proved its capability, firepower and reliability, and it became a complete success in the international weapons market. Most NATO countries now have larger numbers of MLRS in their inventories. To replace the obsolete M163 Vulcan 20mm air defense system, the air defense artillery regiments in the US heavy divisions were equipped with the Bradley Stinger Fighting Vehicle. This tank is very similar to the Bradley and has only slight modifications in the interior of the vehicle. Based today on the M2A2 Bradley, the Stinger air defense missile squad, which comprises two soldiers and the shoulder-fired Stinger, can follow the armored units under armor protection. In the future, the M6 Linebacker will replace the Stinger Bradley. Instead of the TOW 2 launcher box, the Linebacker has a four-round Stinger launcher, and the crew can operate completely under armor protection.

Another Bradley version will be the M7 FIST (Fire Support Team), which replaces the M981 FIST-V in the artillery observer and laser marker role. The US Army's requirements for this M7 vehicle is for more than 300 vehicles based on the M2A2 ODS Bradley.

The introduction of the new M4 Command and Control Vehicle (C2V) is still in progress and is a giant step forward in modern leadership of armored units. The M4 should replace the M577 in the armored units in a ratio of one M4 to two M577s.

The XM5 Electronic Fighting Vehicle System Carrier (X = experimental) is still in the trial phase. But in this case, the vehicle is only the box for storing the most modern military intelligence and electronic technology.

With the introduction of more and more weapon systems based on Bradley components or parts, the standardization in the US Army's fleet of vehicles has increased. Unfortunately, after the succesful Gulf War of 1991, the defense budget was considerably reduced and reorganized. As a result, the future of some planned projects is still uncertain.

During the annual exercise series REFORGER in the winter of 1990, Exercise "Centurion Shield" was held in Bavaria in southern Germany. This was the first time the new M3A2 CFV had taken part in a large-scale maneuver. (Peter Siebert)

An M3A2 CFV Bradley from 1st US ID, 3rd Bn, 34th Armored Rgt featuring "Gold Forces" markings. The new Bradleys in the A2 version were delivered with the foldable rubber screen fitted around the vehicle. As requirements of the European and South Korean theatre in the Cold War, the capability for swimming was requested because of the many small rivers and lakes in these areas. (Peter Siebert)

The production of the upgraded M2A2/M3A2 Bradley began in the spring of 1988. The frontline troops of the 3rd US ID and the 3rd Brigade, 1st US ID in West Germany were equipped in priority with the new tanks in 1989/90. First, the HQ company of mechanized infantry and armor battalions received the new M3A2 Bradley for their scout platoons. But the scouts were not satisfied with the huge Bradley. Prior to Operation "Desert Storm", light Hummer trucks (HMMWV) had replaced the M3A2 CFV in the scout platoons. This photo shows an M3A2 CFV from 3-34 AR, 1st US ID. (Walter Böhm)

Due to progress in the Soviet anti-tank and anti-armor ammunition and missile technology, the main focus of the Bradley upgrading program was better survivability for the crew. Here an M3A2 CFV Bradley of 1st Bn, 16th INF, 1st US ID is fitted with a plastic screen near the driver's hatch to give protection against rain, snow and dirt. (Walter Böhm)

In 1987, the German *Bundeswehr* and the US Army agreed on a new camouflage scheme for all tactical military vehicles. This new NATO 3-tone camouflage is based on three colors: Bronze-green (RAL 6031), Leather-brown (RAL 8027) and Black (RAL 9021). All new M2A2/M3A2 Bradleys from the FMC Corporation in San Jose, California (now United Defense LP) are painted in the new colors when they leave the production line. (Walter Böhm)

During Operation "Desert Storm", the Bradley played a key role. Prior to the start of the ground war in February 1991, all of the nearly 2200 Bradleys were shipped to Saudi Arabia. Six hundred ninety-two of them in the A2 version came from the POMCUS storage site in Europe or straight from the FMC assembly line in San Jose. (US Army)

In early December, 1990, the "Dragoons" (nickname of 2nd Cavalry Regiment) began arriving in Saudi Arabia by ship from Germany, then moved into the intermediate staging area at Inbail. Beginning on 18 December, the regiment moved to the desert, setting up in TAA Seminole. There, the regiment acclimated to the desert and concentrated on individual training. (US Army)

2nd CAV ("Toujours Pret"), spearhead of the 7th "Jayhawk" Corps. As the airwar began, the 2nd CAV began to trade its M3 CFV Bradleys for the new M2A2 infantry fighting vehicles. The photo shows the restoration of the all the equipment from the old M3A0 version into the brand new M2A2. It was unusual to equip a cavalry unit with an M2A2 (infantry) Bradley, but at this time there were not enough M3A2 CFVs available. Notice the bumper code "VII 2CAV" on the old M3A0 Bradley; the new M2A2 had no signs at this time. During the 100-hour war, the Bradley crews used the 25mm gun as their primary weapon against Iraqi infantry and hostile light vehicles. It was reported that the Bradleys of the 3rd US AD used 10,214 25mm rounds, but only 101 TOW anti-tank missiles. (US Army)

In late January 1991, the regiment moved to forward assembly area Richardson, southwest of Hafar Al Batin. Here it held a regimental command post exercise, a war game and combined arm rehearsals. The Bradley cavalry version has an ammunition stock of 10 TOW missiles (plus two ready in the launcher), 1200 25mm rounds for the Bushmaster gun, plus 300 already loaded in the gun. Additionally, there were 3400 rounds for the M60 machine gun and 1680 rounds for the crew's M16A1 rifles. (US Army)

The 2nd CAV crossed the border with its new M2A2 Bradleys through the 43 lanes the engineers cut, with the 4th Squadron (Aviation) in the lead. Two ground squadrons, the 2nd and 3rd, followed closely behind. The 2nd Cavalry Regiment "Dragoons" advanced 30 kilometers (19 miles) and then stopped at phase line "Bud" for the night. (US Army)

A wartime-equipped Bradley from D Troop, 2nd CAV, during Operation "Desert Storm". This M2A2 IFV is fully packed with the crew's gear, MREs, ammunition boxes, additional TOW missiles in wooden boxes, spare parts, and water and oil canisters around the turret and hull. At the beginning of Operation "Desert Storm", the 2nd CAV was under order of the 7th US Armored Corps to scout below the former Iraq-Kuwait border where the units of the Iraqi Republican Guard divisions were now lined up. During the follow-up to the Battle of 73 Easting, the units of 7th US Armored Corps destroyed much of the Iraqi Republican Guard divisions. (US Army)

Snapshot of a fully packed M2A2 Bradley from the 7th US Armored Corps. Of a total of 2200 Bradley fighting vehicles deployed to the desert, there were nearly 1000 of the A2 standard. Most of these new M2A2/M3A2 Bradleys were in units of the 3rd Armored Cavalry Regiment (belonging to the 18th Airborne Corps) and 2nd Armored Cavalry Regiment (belonging to the 7th Armored Corps). (US Army)

This photo, which was taken during an NTC exercise in California, shows three different Bradley versions. In front is an M3A2 CFV. The vehicles together are both A0 standard, while the vehicle in the background is an A1 version with the larger turret basket. (Greg Stewart)

M3A2 CFV Bradley of Headquarters Company, 3rd Armored CAV Regiment (ACR) wearing large tactical numbers on the side skirts as a part of training at NTC after Operation "Desert Storm" in 1991. The 3rd ACR prefers the use of letters for markings instead of the other battle markings (a number in combination with an angular symbol) used in many USAEUR units. (Greg Stewart)

This M3A2 CFV is fitted with extra water canisters on its side skirts. After "Desert Storm", crews became aware of the advantage of having additional water when they operate in a desert climate. Iraq or NTC, the heat is the same. The bigger turret basket allows crewmembers to put their gear in the basket, thus creating more space inside the vehicle. (Greg Stewart)

An M3A2 CFV Bradley with the typical markings of 3rd ACR in the Mojave Desert in October of 1991. The markings on the front of the hull indicate that the vehicle belongs to the HQ Squadron. Notice the "Spinning Vee" on the TOW launcher. This Bradley was fitted with the MILES training gear, including gunfire simulator and strobe light for the main gun, an orange "hit" light on the turret, and sensor tapes around the vehicle. (Greg Stewart)

The Bradley Fighting Vehicle offers an armored, fully tracked, fighting vehicle that has superior cross-country mobility, mounted firepower, protection against artillery and small arms threats, and enhanced situational awareness. Here we see an M3A2 CFV Bradley of 1-1 CAV during live fire exercise "Dragoon Thunder 97" in Grafenwöhr, Germany. (Walter Böhm)

The Bradley is able to close with and destroy enemy forces in support of mounted and dismounted infantry and cavalry operations. Seen here are dismounted infantry of 2-6 INF, CMTC Hohenfels, Germany. (Peter Siebert)

Two generations: M113 and M2A2 IFV ODS Bradley. The old M113 APC protects infantrymen only during transport. During combat, the soldiers must leave the APC. During the Vietnam War, the troops considered this the main flaw of the M113. Armored troops need agile and well-protected vehicles. With the introduction of the Bradley IFV/CFV, the American soldiers got a suitable vehicle for a successful fight based on a fast, well-protected, well-armed, and up-to-date vehicle. It is also a weapon system with the capability to protect dismounted infantrymen. (Walter Böhm)

"Comanche Country". Patch of Comanche Troop, 1st Squadron, 1st Cavalry Regiment. (Walter Böhm)

Combined Arms Live Fire Exercise (CALFEX): M3A2 CFV Bradley and M1A1HA Abrams of Comanche Troop, 1-1 CAV at Range 301, Training Area Grafenwöhr. Range 301 is the largest, most modern range in Europe. After the introduction of the new M1 Abrams and M2/M3 Bradley weapon systems in 1985, the upgraded Range 301 was handed over to the troops. Since that time, computer-based training systems with fixed and movable targets and the entire control system have been continually updated. (Walter Böhm)

Abrams and Bradley: the strongest pair of fighting vehicles in the world. Most of the time, mechanized infantry units will operate together with tanks. Mechanized infantry fight dismounted or from on board their Bradley. Battle tanks, mechanized infantry, and cavalry units support each other and are interdependent. The Bradley weapon system has the capability to be teamed up with the M1A1/A2 Abrams MBT. (Walter Böhm)

The Bradley's main weapon system is the fully stablized M242 Bushmaster 25mm chain gun from Boeing Company. The effective fighting distance for the Bushmaster is up to 3000 meters (3280 yards). (Walter Böhm)

The dual-feed M242 Bushmaster, which is fitted with 300-round magazines, can use the Oerlikon 25mm rounds, as well as the American M790 ammunition series, including M791 TP-T, TP-DST (Target Practice Discarding Sabot Tracer), and the new M919 APFSDS-T (Armor Piercing, Fin-Stabilized, Discarding Sabot Tracer). Here an M3A2 CFV Bradley from Bandit Troop, 1-1 CAV fires flare rounds during Tank Table VIII live fire training in "Graf". (Walter Böhm)

The usual mix of ammunition in the ready magazine is 75 rounds of armor piercing (AP) and 225 rounds of high explosive (HE). The Bradley initially used the M791 armor piercing discarding sabot (APDS) projectile with a tungsten carbide core. The improved M919 depleted uranium fin-stabilzed projectile became available in limited quantities in 1991. (Walter Böhm)

The coaxial M240C 7.62mm machine gun is located next to the M242 chain gun. The magazine holds 800 7.62mm rounds. The two small boxes alongside the main gun on the turret are smoke grenade stowage boxes. The armored flap over the gunner's sight is in the raised position. Notice the turret's additional armor plates. (Walter Böhm)

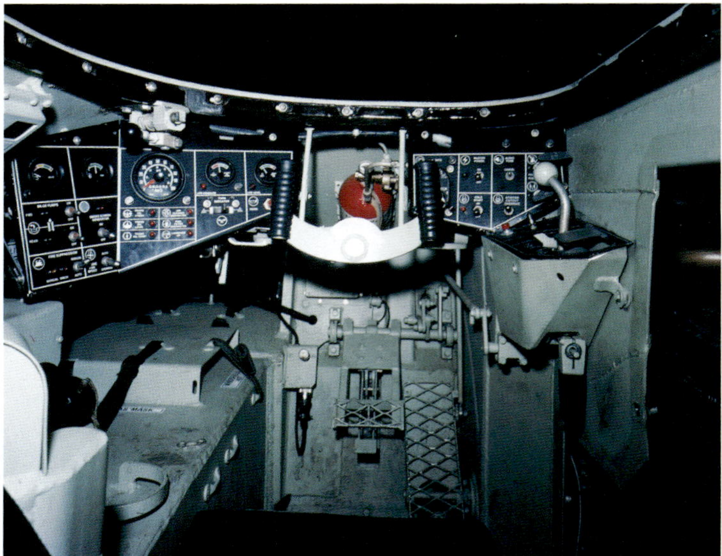

The driver's compartment in the Bradley is spacious and well laid out, and all the switches are located within easy reach. The engine compartment is located to the right of the driver. (Greg Stewart)

Compared with other armored vehicles, the driver's compartment in the Bradley is fitted with a large hatch, which opens in the vertical direction. For good sighting, it is fitted with four periscopes. (Walter Böhm)

Both the Bradley commander and gunner can fire all turret weapon systems. The gunner can select a firing rate from single shot to automatic fire with a ratio of 100 or 200 rounds per minute. This photo shows the tank commander's position with the turret traverse control stick on the right side of the turret. The commander's sight is connected to the gunner's main sight. (Peter Siebert)

The gunner is located on the left side of the turret. He can use periscopes for side view and the combined day/night thermal sight for main observation and tracking. (Peter Siebert)

"Shark in an Ambush". For combat against tanks, the M2A2/M3A2 Bradley is equipped with the twin-tube TOW 2B ATGM missile launcher system. The TOW 2B weapon system is capable of defeating hostile armored vehicles at a range of up to 3750 meters (4100 yards). The two thermal beacons on the launcher allow for missile tracking and guidance through fog, mist, dust, smoke, and in daytime or nighttime conditions. This M2A2 IFV Bradley with an erected TOW 2B launcher has taken up an ambush position during training at CMTC Hohenfels, Germany. The vehicle belongs to 1-36 INF, 1st US AD. (Walter Böhm)

"Refuel on the Move (ROM)". The M2A2/M3A2 Bradley has a fuel capacity of 662 liters (175 gallons) of JP8 Fuel (military specification for "diesel"), giving the tank a cruising range of up to 483 km (300 miles). Notice the temporary white chalk stencelling "Pork and Beans Forever: 1000 Hit Score" on this M3A2 CFV Bradley from 1st Squadron, 1st CAV Rgt. (Walter Böhm)

Bradley fire protection system. The M2A2/M3A2 Bradley has an improved fire extinguishing system, with one 3.2kg Halon fire extinguisher mounted in the engine compartment, two portable Halon fire extinguishers for manual use by the crew, and two automatic 2.3kg Halon fire extinguishers in the rear personnel compartment. With this equipment, most fires inside the tank, especially those in the ammunition storage and the fuel tanks, can be extinguished before they become dangerous. (Walter Böhm)

OPFOR Bradley. The Bradley's hull is relatively high, with a sloping front and a horizontal hull roof. The A2 version features improved suspension. The fire ports on the rear ramp were closed in the M3A2 CFV. (Walter Böhm)

"Composed Behavior". An M3A2 CFV from Charlie-Rock Troop, 1-4 CAV sits in front of the ruins of the Hopfenoher church at the training area at Grafenwöhr. The M3A2 carries a crew of three along with two observers located beneath the rear cargo hatch. The cargo hatch is fitted with additional periscopes for a better vision to enhance the scouting role of the CFV. The M2/M3 Bradley carriage has six roadwheels, with a larger gap between the third and fourth wheel. Two return rollers are on each side, with the drive sprocket in the front and the idler in the rear. (Walter Böhm)

The M2A2 Infantry Fighting Vehicle (IFV) carries a crew of three (commander, driver and gunner), along with six soldiers. Superior performance and mobility enables the M2A2 to deliver its infantry squad to the mission area, where they can dismount and fight. Seen in this photo is an infantry squad from 2-6 INF during MOUT training in Baumholder, Germany. (Walter Böhm)

To honor their roots in the Indian Wars, the members of the modern US Army's cavalry units wear black stetsons. The colors of cavalry units have been red and white from that time until today. (Walter Böhm)

To support its role in mounted cavalry operations, the M3A2 has an interior arrangement that includes additional stowage space for supplies and ammunition to sustain combat operations. (Greg Stewart)

The main purposes for the M2A2/M3A2 upgrading were 1) better protection by internal armor for key components and 2) additional armor plates on the front and side of the hull and turret. Also included are better passive protection against fire and explosion by restowing the ammunition; spall liners; and mounting provisions for an updated vehicle smoke screening. (Walter Böhm)

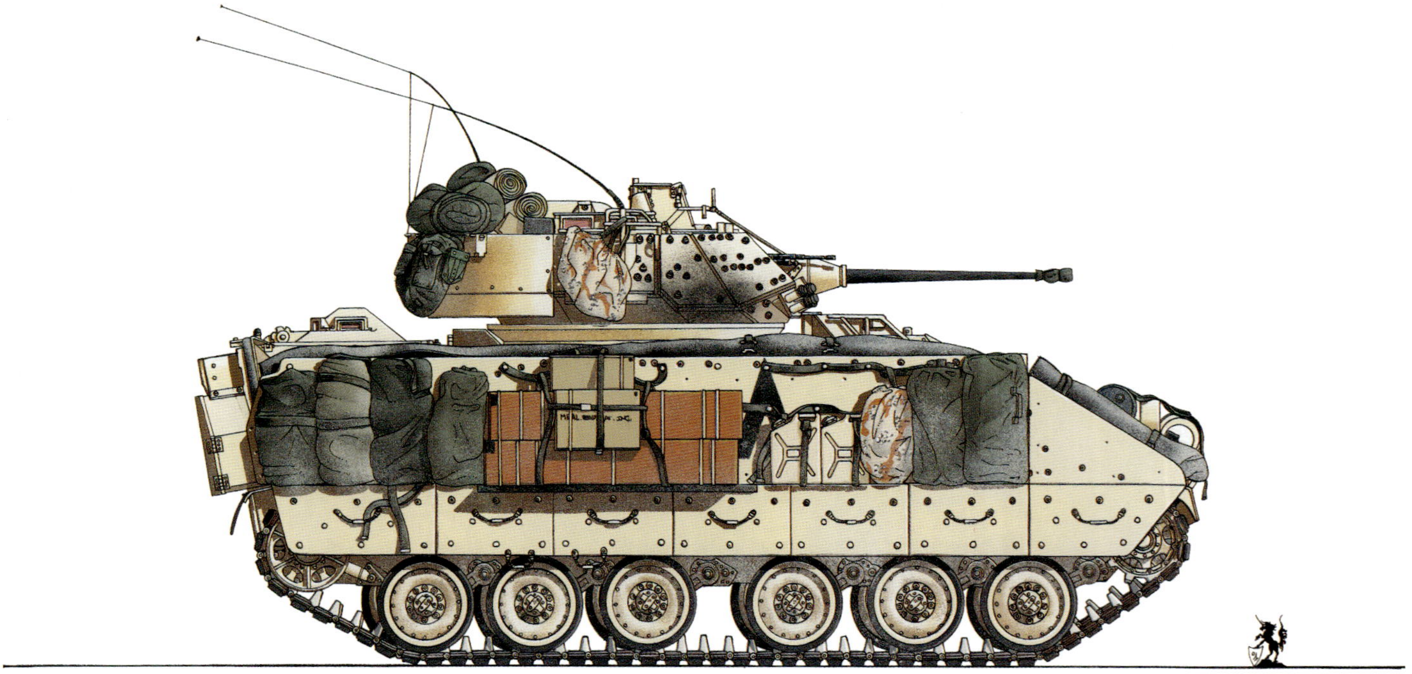

M2A2 IFV Bradley, D Troop, 2nd Squadron, 2nd Cavalry Regiment, Assembly Area Richardson, Iraq/Kuwait border, January 1991

The reconnaissance units of the VII US Armored Corps were hastily equipped with the brand new M2A2 IFV Bradley just before the Gulf War's ground offensive began. A few days before the beginning of the ground war operations, the crews mounted their baggage, extra ammunition and combat rations on the outside of their vehicles. Because of this, the coalition markings, the inverted "V" (chevron) was nearly completely covered up and cannot be easily recognized.

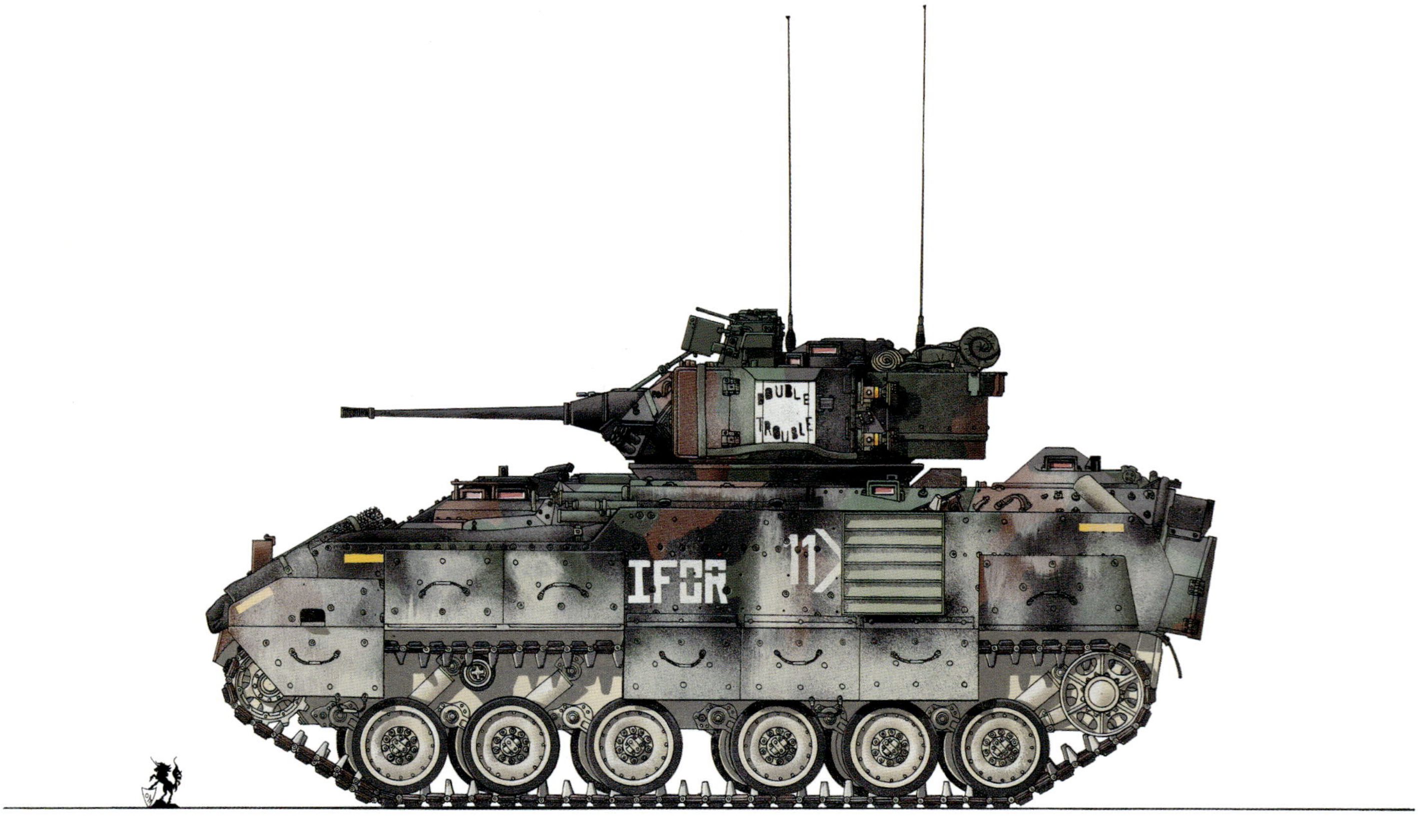

M2A2 IFV Bradley, A Company, 3rd Squadron, 5th Cavalry Regiment, Brcko, northern Bosnia, September 1996

All Bradleys taking part in Operation "Joint Endevour" in the former Yugoslavia were marked with the "IFOR" stencilling and had Friend/Foe panels on the hull and the turret. The name "Double Trouble" refers to the deadly effect of the dual-tube TOW launcher. The tactical marking "11" with the arrow pointing to the right represents 2nd Platoon, A Company, 3-5 CAV, which was under operation order of 1st Brigade, 1st US AD.

M2A2 IFV Bradley, 2nd Battalion, 6th Infantry Regiment, CMTC Hohenfels, Germany, 1997

This M2A2 IFV Bradley of 1st Platoon, C Company (nickname "Rock") took part in Exercise "Iron Star 97" during the rotation of the 1st US Armored Division at CMTC Hohenfels. In order to avoid damage to or blockage of the tracks and road wheels with dirt and mud, the rear section of the side skirt is turned upwards. Note the insignia "Death with Scythe" on the TOW launcher; this is the insignia of 1st Platoon, C Company.

M3A2 ODS CFV Bradley, 1st Squadron, 4th Cavalry Regiment, Altzirkendorf, February 2001

The 1st Squadron, 4th Cavalry Regiment received their first new ODS Bradleys in August 2000. During Exercise "Troop Challenge 01", the vehicles were relatively new and wore additional "battle markings" on the hull. This "Quarterhorse" Bradley is fitted with the MILES II training system equipment. On the eyelets on the sides of the hull, the crew can fix additional gear and equipment. A water canister is normally stowed behind the rubber flap on the front end of the skirt.

More improvements on the A2 version of the Bradley were the upgraded and reinforced suspension, drive train and tracks, and a ballistic shroud for the commander's back-up sight. (Walter Böhm)

The M2A2/M3A2 Bradley is transportable by track, rail, ship, or aircraft. Here M2A2 IFV Bradleys from A Company, 2-6 INF (nickname "Regulars") are carried on freight cars of the German *Bundesbahn* near the German town of Parsberg after the CMTC Hohenfels rotation in March of 2000. (Walter Böhm)

The Bradley can be airlifted by C-141, C-5 and C-17 aircraft. This M2A2 belongs to the 3rd ID (mech) as a part of the 18th Airborne Corps. It is on its way to being transported by a McDonnell Douglas C-17A Globemaster III of 437th Airlift Wing. The 18th Airborne Corps is part of the US Army Rapid Reaction Forces. These units are capable of being deployed anywhere in the world within 24 hours. (Carl Schulze)

During Operation "Swift Crossing 98", two M2A2 IFVs from 1st Bn, 18th INF crossed the Main River near Schonungen, Germany, on a Ribbon ridge raft belonging to 502nd Engineer Company, 565th Engineer Battalion. The Ribbon bridge rafts have a capacity for up to 70 tons. (Walter Böhm)

"Wings for a Bradley". During Exercise "JTFEX 96/Royal Dragon", a practice for the rapid deployment of a brigade task force, 3rd ID (mech) was trained with the support of Air Mobility Command (AMC) using C-17A Globemaster IIIs based at Charleston AFB/South Carolina. (Carl Schulze)

A Bradley company operations center. Bradley Bravo Warrior and the company commander's vehicle from B Company, 1-36 INF (nickname "Spartans"), 1st US AD were connected with tarpaulins and turned into a company operations center. The temporary tarpaulin can be removed quickly but gives the soldiers the necessary protection against rain in their assembly area at CMTC Hohenfels. Nobody knows if, or when, the new M4 Command and Control vehicle (C2V) would be delivered to the USAEUR units in Europe. (Walter Böhm)

The battalion patch of the "Spartans" of 1st Bn, 36th Inf Rgt. The unit's motto is "Deeds not Words". (Walter Böhm)

A weapon interlock is integrated and activated when the hatches open. In 2001, there was a total of 421 CFVs in the US Army units. One of them is this CFV of 1-1 CAV, which is based in Germany. (Walter Böhm)

"Deer Hunter". This Bradley's crew found some antlers in the woods of CMTC Hohenfels and affixed them as a trophy to their Bradley M2A2 IFV of 2-6 INF. But during the CMTC rotation, they fell victim to the OPFOR anti-tank teams. (Walter Böhm)

"Combat Recovery". An M88A1 recovery tank pulls a broken-down M2A2 IFV Bradley of 2-6 INF on the Hohenburg road during a CMTC rotation in February 2000. To protect the M242 weapon, the barrel of the Bushmaster gun was removed. (Walter Böhm)

"Broken Track". The crewmembers of "Charlie 13", 2-6 INF try to repair a tread track with the help of another Bradley during a STX day at CMTC Hohenfels. The Bradley track is 533mm (21 inches) wide. (Walter Böhm)

"Wait for the Eighty-eight". The rocky soil at CMTC Hohenfels is typical of the terrain in the low mountain areas of central Europe. During a CMTC rotation, all kinds of material are pushed to their limits, like this M2A2 IFV Bradley. The crew can't solve the problem; they really need a recovery tank. (Walter Böhm)

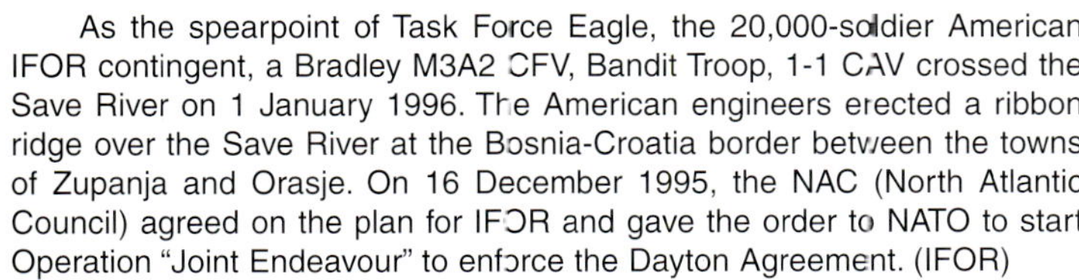

As the spearpoint of Task Force Eagle, the 20,000-soldier American IFOR contingent, a Bradley M3A2 CFV, Bandit Troop, 1-1 CAV crossed the Save River on 1 January 1996. The American engineers erected a ribbon ridge over the Save River at the Bosnia-Croatia border between the towns of Zupanja and Orasje. On 16 December 1995, the NAC (North Atlantic Council) agreed on the plan for IFOR and gave the order to NATO to start Operation "Joint Endeavour" to enforce the Dayton Agreement. (IFOR)

An M2A2 IFV Bradley belonging to the "Black Knights" of 3CAV5 blocks a bridge on the road leading from Brko to the Save River, the natural border between Serbian and Croatian territory. IFOR established checkpoints on all important crossroads and intersections. (Walter Böhm)

"Bold Thrower" in Brko, northern Bosnia. An M2A2 IFV Bradley (behind barbed wire) from A Company, Task Force 3CAV5, gives protection to an IFOR checkpoint in the Bosnian village of Brko. This village was the center of fighting in the narrow Posanvia Corridor, which was under the control of the Serbian forces. The Bradleys were deployed on a platoon scale when protecting an IFOR checkpoint. (Walter Böhm)

M2A2 IFV Bradley in Forward Operating Base (FOB) McGovern in northern Bosnia. The base camp of Task Force 3CAV5 was located in the center of the "Zone of Seperation" (ZOS) at the end of 1996. The former front line, today it is the border between the former enemies. FOB McGovern was named in honor of an officer of 3CAV5 that was killed in the Korean War. During preparation for Operation "Joint Endeavour", most armored vehicles were fitted with so-called Identification Friend/Foe Panels (IFF). These plates make it easier to identify friendly (IFOR) vehicles by means of thermal sights. The plates appear as dark squares that contrast with the light (because of the heat) silhouette of the vehicles. (Walter Böhm)

Some M2A2 IFVs of B Company, Task Force 3CAV5 are parked beside a damaged silo in FOB McGovern. Notice the IFOR (Implementation Force) stencilling near the IFF panel. FOB McGovern was home to up to 800 soldiers by the end of 1996. The area was protected by combat vehicles, sand walls, observation towers, and miles of barbed wire. Most of the soldiers belonged to A Company ("Raiders"), B Company ("Warriors"), D Company ("Destroyers"), and HHQ Company ("Highlanders") from 3CAV5 ("Black Knights"). (Walter Böhm)

An M88A1 recovery tank pulls the powerpack out of a Bradley at FOB McGovern. The Cummins VTA-903T engine in the A2 version provides 600 hp and has a 14.8-liter cubic capacity. (Walter Böhm)

The Bradley powerpack is a combination of the Cummins VTA-903 T engine and a General Dynamics Defense System HMPT-500 hydromechanical transmission. (Walter Böhm)

On 20 December 1996, IFOR was replaced by the SFOR (Stabilization Force). The troops were restructured and reduced from 60,000 down to a total of 30,000 soldiers. But one threat and risk remained omnipresent for the units – mines! This unique picture shows a Pearson Mine Roller (MR) mounted to an M2A2 IFV Bradley from 2nd Bn, 2nd Inf Rgt, 3rd Bde, 1st US ID, near the village of Brko. For use on an M2/M3 Bradley, the Pearson Mine Roller has 700mm- (27.5-inch) wide rollerpacks and a weight of 1150 kg (2536 lb). It can operate at a speed up to 50 km/h (31 mph). (Carl Schulze)

The rear view of the same Bradley from 2-2 INF with the Pearson MR, which is shown here during a mine clearing job near Brko. The side skirts are mounted upwards, with only the middle panel remaining in the regular position to show the SFOR lettering. (Carl Schulze)

In March 1997, HHC 3rd Brigade and 2-2 INF deployed to Bosnia-Herzegovina for Operation "Joint Guard", where they saw action during the riots in Brko. In October 1997, the 3rd Brigade redeployed to its home base in Vilseck, Germany, where it prepared for the next call to arms. This photo offers another rare view, an M2A2 IFV Bradley from A Company, 2-2 INF (based in FOB McGovern) equipped with the Surface Mine Plough 1. The SMP 1 weighs 1250 kg (2756 lb) and can clean a 3.56-meter (3.90-yard) wide track. (Carl Schulze)

On 15 June 1999, M2A2 IFV Bradleys from 1-6 INF, based temporarily in Macedonia, crossed the border into Kosovo. Along with M1A1HA Abrams from 1-35 Armored Rgt, they made up Task Force Falcon, part of the International Security Force Kosovo (KFOR). KFOR was tasked with enforcing UN Resolution 1244. Here an M2A2 Bradley from D Company, 1-6 INF is seen en route to Gujilane/Kosovo. (Carl Schulze)

An M2A2 IFV Bradley from 1-6 INF protects KFOR's main invasion route from Macedonia to Kosovo. The 1-6 INF was subordinate to 1st US ID (Task Force Falcon) for the Kosovo deployment. Task Force Falcon is the US portion of KFOR. Its area of responsibility is the southeastern corner of Kosovo, roughly running from the border of Macedonia to Urosevac and northeast to the Serbian border, beyond the town of Kosovska-Kamenica. Both major US Army camps in Kosovo are named for 1st Infantry Division soldiers: SSgt James Bondsteel, who was awarded the Medal of Honor for gallantry in Vietnam and 1st Lt. Jimmie Monteith, who was awarded the Medal of Honor for gallantry on D-Day. (Carl Schulze)

This Task Force Tiger M2A2 ODS IFV Bradley from 1-26 INF, 1st US ID is posted near Moglia to control the flood of refugees returning to Kosovo. This area was under the control of the American-led Multinational Brigade East. The 1-26 INF was the first USAEUR unit to be issued the new ODS Bradley. (Carl Schulze)

ODS Bradley of Task Force Tiger in the Vitina Obstina/Kosovo region. Task Force Tiger was led by the 1-77 AR (nickname "Steel Tiger"). It has the following structure: HQ Company, Support Company, A and C Company, 1-77 AR (with a total of 28 M1A1HAs), one company from 1-26 INF, one company of 3-504 Parachute Infantry Regiment, a battery from 1-7 FA (M109A6 Paladin), C Company of 9th Engineers Bn, and air support by 2-1 AVN Bn. (Carl Schulze)

An M2A2 ODS Bradley from A Company, 1-26 INF on patrol in the mountains seperating Macedonia from Kosovo in the southern part of Task Force Tiger's Area Of Responsibility (AOR). Its mission is to stop the illegal arms traffic across the border. (Carl Schulze)

As a regular cavalry regiment, the 1-4 CAV has about 41 Cavalry Fighting Vehicles (CFV) in the unit. "Troop Challenge 01" was the first exercise in which 1-4 CAV operated the new ODS standard vehicle. (Walter Böhm)

The crew of this Bradley of B Troop, 1-4 CAV navigate their brand new tank through the small town of Altzirkendorf, north of Grafenwöhr, in February 2001. The 1-4 CAV, 1st US ID received their first improved M3A2 ODS tanks in August 2000. (Walter Böhm)

"Troop Challenge 01" tested every troop in battle techniques, handling the new ODS Bradleys, and cooperation among the squadron's main elements. Dismounted teams in the woods, together with M3A2 ODS and M1A1HA mechanized fighting vehicles, were supported and guided by OH-58D Warrior choppers. (Walter Böhm)

The freeland exercise "Troop Challenge 01" was a treat for the troops of 1-4 CAV. The enviroment of real small towns, farms and civilians made the exercise more realistic than the usual training in CMTC Hohenfels or NTC California. (Walter Böhm)

This photo of an M3A2 ODS CFV Bradley was taken in the nearby town of Kirchenthumbach, Germany. To reinforce the M3A2 ODS against HEAT charges, RAFAEL Defense Systems was given the order for 175 ERA kits. This modular reactive armor kits consist of 105 ERA plates to cover the front of the hull, the sides and the turret. (Walter Böhm)

American-German scout team. The 1-4 CAV is the reconnaissance unit for the 1st US ID. This American unit, which is based in Schweinfurt, Germany, has a partnership program with the German *Bundeswehr*'s *Panzeraufklärungsbattaillon* 12, which is based in Ebern. Seen here is a combined scout team with 1-4 CAV M3A2 ODS and a *Spähpanzer* Luchs from PzAufklBtl.12. The mission of 1-4 CAV as a scout for 1st US ID is to be alert, deploy, prepare for combat operations, and conduct reconnaissance and security operations. (Walter Böhm)

The maneuver area with its small towns and hilly terrain make successful communication a challenge for the crews of the scattered vehicles. (Walter Böhm)

Today's US Army cavalry units are still ready for a fight. With their mix of M1A1HA Abrams MBTs, Bradley CFVs and multi-role OH-58D Warrior helicopters, the unit can operate relatively independently. They can discover the enemy and stop or hold him until reinforcement becomes necessary. US-based CAV are reinforced with one battery of M109A6 Paladin howitzers. (Walter Böhm)

FTX "Troop Challenge 01" provided realistic training. The 1-4 CAV trains at CMTC Hohenfels many times a year, so crews know the terrain and operate similarly to their previous rotation. When 1-4 CAV trains "out of the box', it becames a challenge for the crews to find their way in the unknown terrain, whether by day and night, in sun or snow. (Walter Böhm)

The scenario for the “Troop Challenge 01” exercise was variable and could change from a peacekeeping to a wartime mission. For a reconnaissance unit like 1-4 CAV, it is necessary to be flexible and respond quickly when the type of mission changes, especially when faced with a sensitive situation like in the Balkan regions. (Walter Böhm)

The next upgrading for the ODS Bradley is still in progress. Key elements will be a Global Positioning System with a screen, a missile countermeasure device, and a modernized layout for stowage and internal components. (Walter Böhm)

This close-up of a turret shows the components of the MILES II training system, the improved driver's hatch and the additional armor plates on the turret and the front of the hull. (Walter Böhm)

The commander is located on the turret's right side. He is connected to the gunner's Integrated Sight Unit (ISU), a combined day/night thermal sight and fire control system. Beneath the commander you see the thin antennas of the SINCGARS radios (Single Channel Ground and Airborne Radio System). The SINCGARS can use 2320 different frequences between 30 and 87,975 MHz on the VHF band. (Walter Böhm)

ODS stowage improvements. The rear floor plates and stowage are modified in the M3A2 ODS. The two scouts are seated at the left side. The mounts for three AT-4 anti-tank missiles replaced the Dragon and LAW mounts. Under the floorplates there is space for three boxes of 25mm HE ammunition, each with 50 rounds. The inside of the IFV and CFV Bradleys is now painted in FS 24410 Semi-gloss Light Green. (Walter Böhm)

The Bradley's TOW systems were upgraded to take full advantage of the improved types of TOW missile, i.e., the TOW 2, TOW 2A and TOW 2B, on the M2/M3 ODS Bradley. The TOW 2B ATGM is a wire-controlled weapon operated by the gunner. The elevation of the launcher is between –20 to 0 degrees. The new dual hollow-head warhead can penetrate armor up to 90cm (35.5 inches) under ideal conditions. (Walter Böhm)

The two scouts riding in the CFV version can leave the vehicle via a door in the rear ramp. To the left and right of the ramp are stowage boxes that can hold a variety of things, including ammo boxes, radio cables, rations, etc. While conducting exercises in wooded areas, these boxes are often destroyed, lost, or damaged. (Walter Böhm)

The M2A2/M3A2 Bradley running gear was upgraded with a new style of tracks similar to the "Big Foot" tracks on the M1A1HA Abrams. These have larger rubber pads to increase track life during peacetime on-road travel. (Walter Böhm)

To reduce the number of casualities from friendly fire in future conflicts, modern American fighting vehicles will be equipped with the Battlefield Combat Identification System (BCIS). Notice the wire cutter near the driver's hatch and the modified exhaust system on this M3A2 ODS. (Walter Böhm)

Another improvement on the ODS standard is the engine access door; an electro-hydraulic lift mechanism raises and lowers the engine door quickly and easy. The mechanism is controlled from the driver's position. (Walter Böhm)

1/35 M3A2 " BRADLEY " +ERA

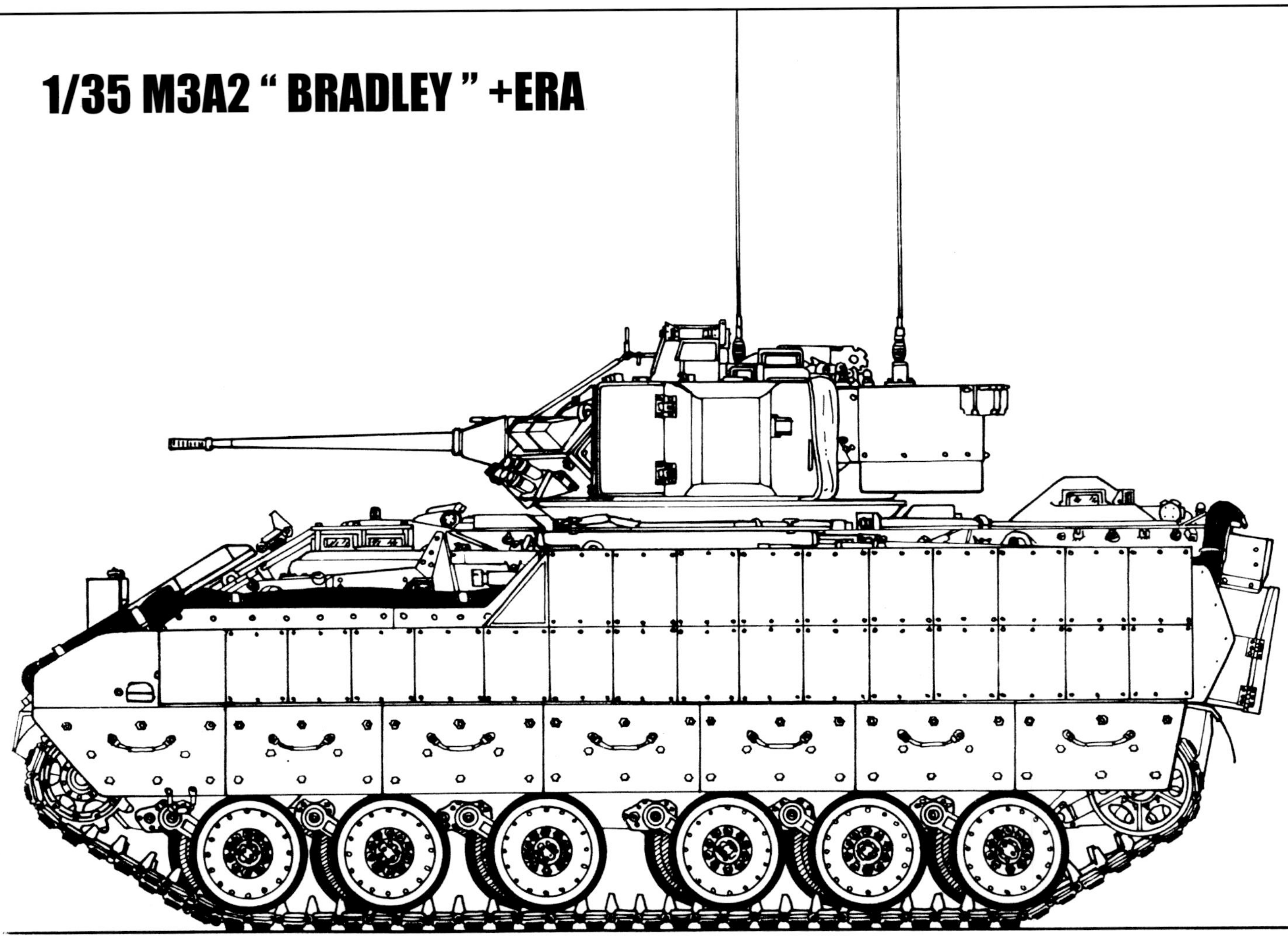

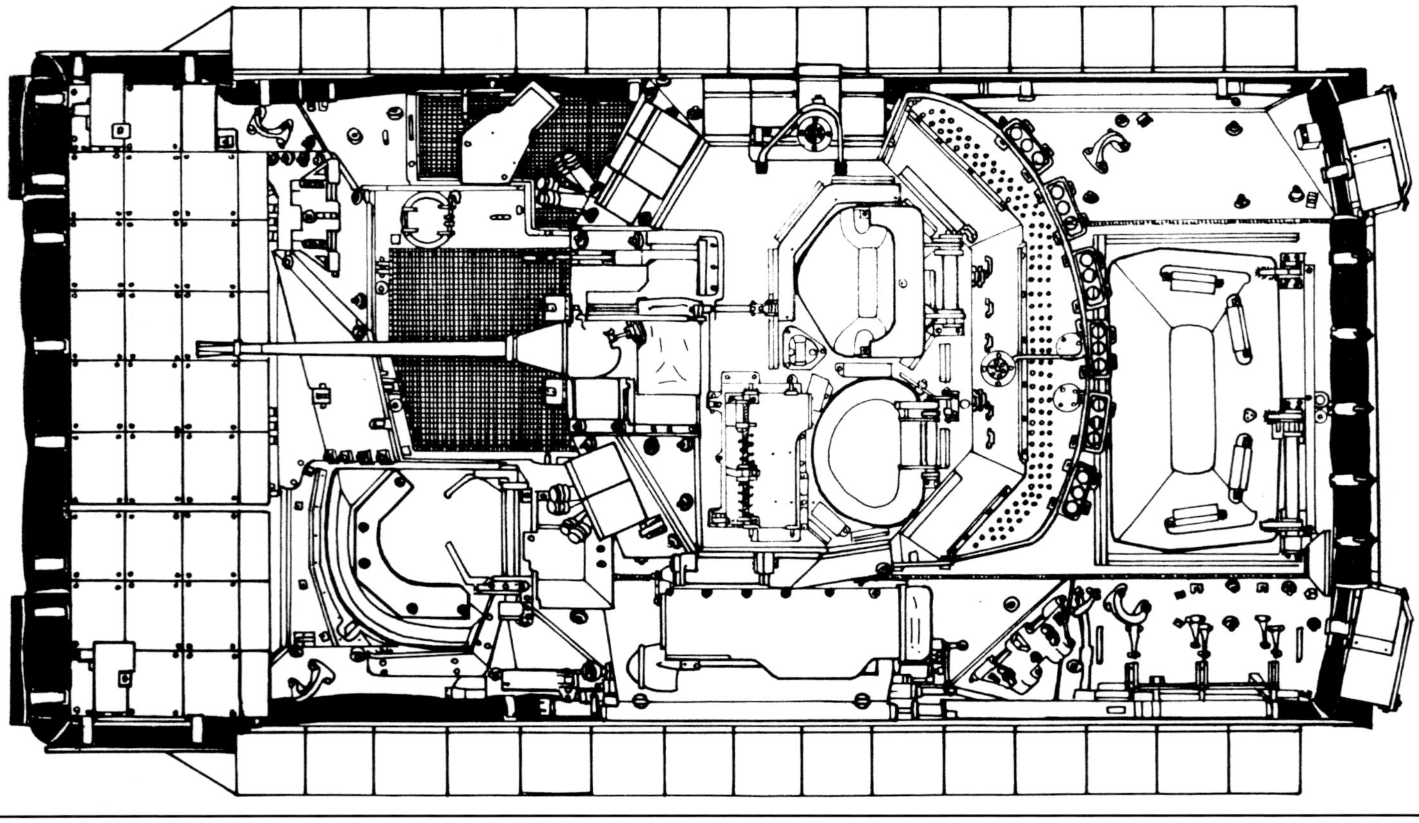

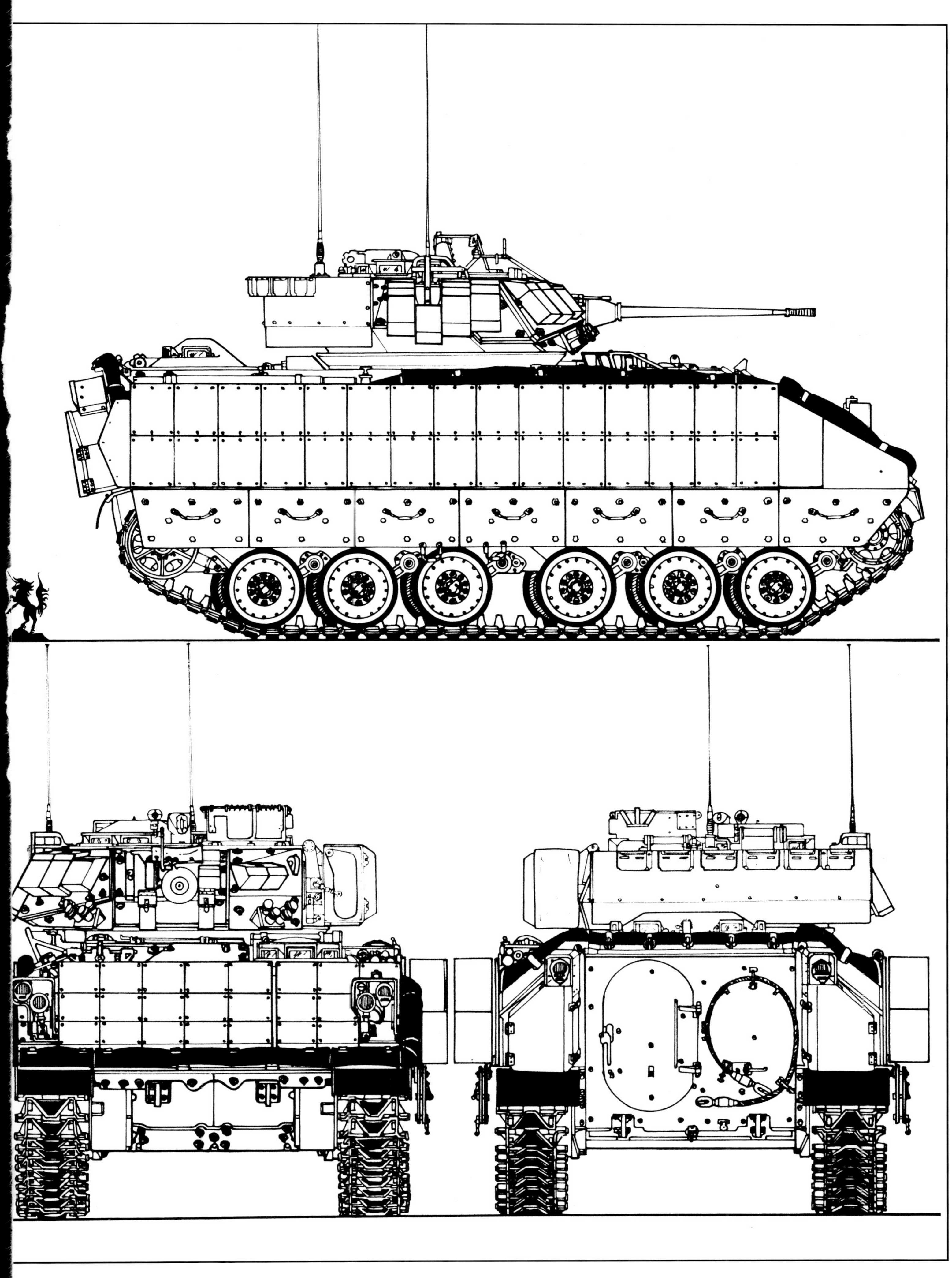

"Armored Cavalry Power". Reconnaissance units scout and observe supported by today's modern electronic systems. A cavalry squadron has a variety of tactical vehicles to choose from. There are 41 M3A2 ODS CFV Bradleys, 27 M1A1HA Abrams MBTs, 16 OH-58D Kiowa Warrior helicopters, and 120mm mortars. The whole squadron has a strength of 730 soldiers. (Walter Böhm)

For better visiual identification of tactical vehicles on the battlefield USAEUR equips its fighting vehicles with so-called "battle markings". The large plate on the rear turret basket is one of these markings. The two numerals and the angle represent the unit and the platoon. Here the number "03" stands for C Troop, 1-4 CAV. The downward angle indicates the third platoon. (Walter Böhm)

The HQ platoon of an Armored Cavalry Regiment has one M3A2 CFV Bradley, one M1A1HA Abrams, one M577A2, and, for the artillery observer's role, one M981 FIST-V. The artillery observer in his M981 FIST-V operates in continous contact with, and as closely as possible to, the squadron commander so he can call for artillery support when necessary. (Walter Böhm)

The orginal TOW missiles fitted to the first model of the Bradley could destroy Soviet-made T-55 and T-62 MBTs. Because newer Soviet battle tanks like the T-64 and T-72 have heavier armor protection, the A1 versions of the Bradley were fitted with the TOW 2 missile system. Packing a larger warhead, this missile could kill newer generations of Soviet main battle tanks. The TOW missile system, unlike the 25mm chain gun, cannot fire on the move. (Walter Böhm)

The NATO 3-tone camouflage scheme has been improved. Today there are new colors used. Called CARC (Chemical Agent Resisting Coating), this paint has a smoother surface that makes it easier to clean or decontaminate the vehicles. Besides the tactical markings, this ODS Bradley vehicle from 1-4 CAV features no more stencilling. (Walter Böhm)

The ODS Bradley's side skirts contain seven seperate steel elements. Each is fitted with two bolts on the hull. To prevent damage to tracks or skirts during peacetime exercises, the crew fits the side skirts upward. Only the two in front remain in their regular place to make it easier for the crew to mount and dismount. (Walter Böhm)

The suspension system, with its 14 inches of vertical clearance and high-performance shock absorbers, enables the Bradley to travel at high speed over rough terrain. Fully packed under combat conditions, the Bradley can accelerate from a standing start to 50km/h (30mph) in less than 22 seconds. (Walter Böhm)

"Search and Destroy". The Bradley's two main weapons, the 25mm chain gun and the coaxial 7.62mm machine gun, are fully stabilized in traverse and elevation. This provides excellent firing accuracy on the move. This is an advantage the Soviet BMP does not have. (Walter Böhm)

The status of the year 2001 program is that the Army will be modifying 1433 A2s to the A2 ODS configuration and preparing to upgrade 1602 A2 vehicles to the new A3 configuration. The First Unit Equipped (FUE) with the A2 ODS standard was the 3rd US ID (mech), based in the USA, during Field Year 1996. (Walter Böhm)

The ODS CFV Bradley's armor offers protection against 95% of all ballistic attacks that can take place on a battlefield when the vehicle operates in the typical CFV role, according to a report by the manufacturer, United Defense LP. (Walter Böhm)

In the event of a failure of the day/night sights, the crew can use the M242 Bushmaster gun's provisional daylight sight. The turret can turn at a maximum of 60 degrees per second. (Walter Böhm)

"Combined Arms Team". The M3A2 ODS CFV Bradley and the M1A1 Abrams MBT comprise the combined arms team. In this team, the CFV's main job is to destroy hostile IFVs and other light armor. In the US Army's heavy division concept, in the future only two combat brigades will be equipped with the ODS standard Bradley. The third brigade will still have older M2A2 vehicles, until the A3 version is delivered. There should be a total of 1647 Bradleys modified to the ODS configuration. (Walter Böhm)

Some minor modifications on the 1-4 CAV ODS CFV Bradley are the improved side skirts, the wire cutter and the easier-to-handle driver's hatch. (Walter Böhm)

The hull of the M2A2/M3A2 ODS is uparmored with spaced laminate steel armor on the side skirts. Add-on armor plates were used to reinforce the upper and lower front glacis, the hull sides and bottom. (Walter Böhm)

The 2nd Dagger Brigade Combat Team of 1st US ID (mech) is headquartered in Schweinfurt, Germany. Its maneuver units are: 1st Bn, 26th INF ("Blue Spade") and 1st Bn, 18th INF ("Dog Face"), both units being equipped with M2A2 ODS IFV Bradley; 1st Bn, 77th Armored Rgt ("Steel Tigers"), fitted with M1A1HA Abrams; 1st Bn, 7th Field Artillery, equipped with M109A6 Paladin; and the 9th Engineer Bn. All brigade units are based in Schweinfurt. (Walter Böhm)

On 24 May 1917, the 2nd Dagger Brigade was first constituted as Headquarters Infantry Brigade of the 1st Expeditionary Division, which was later designated as 1st Division. Following WWII, the Brigade was redesignated as HHQ Company, 2nd Infantry Brigade. In WWII, it operated as 2nd Airborne Infantry Brigade as a part of the Normancy campaign of 1944. In September 1965, the 2nd Brigade deployed to Vietnam. The Brigade returned to Fort Riley in 1969. In 1990, the 2nd Dagger Brigade deployed to Saudi Arabia for Operation "Desert Storm". On 15 February 1996, the 2nd Dagger Brigade came to Schweinfurt as a part of 1st US Infantry Division (mech). (Walter Böhm)

Dagger Brigade's mission is to deploy all or part of the Brigade Combat Team, seperately or as a part of a heavy division, in response to a conflict, whether it be a peace-keeping mission or intense combat, then, on order, to redeploy and prepare for further operations. The motto of the 2nd Dagger Brigade is: "No mission too difficult, no sacrifice too great. Duty first". (Walter Böhm)

“Fighting First”. One legend has emerged in answer to the question, “How did the Big Red One patch originate?” One story has it that during WWI, the division’s supply trucks were of English manufacture, so the American drivers painted a huge “1” on these trucks to distinguish them from the trucks made by the other allies. Later, division engineers carried the measure a step farther by sewing a red patch on their sleeves on which was placed the number “1” for 1st US Infantry Division. Thus, the “Big Red One” was born. (Walter Böhm)

Close-up of the “Big Red One” division patch painted on an ODS Bradley TOW launcher of 1-26 INF. The 1st US ID (mech) has four brigades: the 1st Brigade is located in Fort Riley, USA; the 2nd Brigade in Schweinfurt, Germany; the 3rd Brigade in Vilseck, Germany; and the 4th Aviation Brigade is headquartered in Katterbach, Germany. (Walter Böhm)

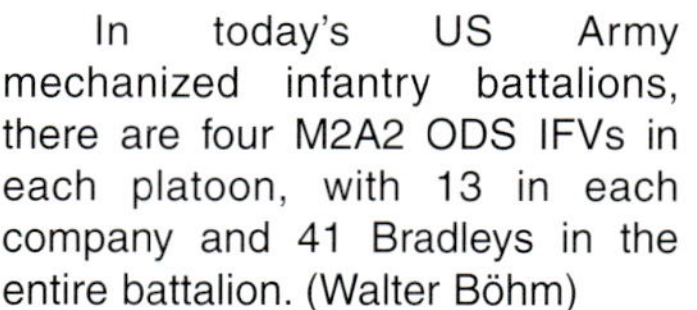

In today’s US Army mechanized infantry battalions, there are four M2A2 ODS IFVs in each platoon, with 13 in each company and 41 Bradleys in the entire battalion. (Walter Böhm)

In the 7th US Army Combat Maneuver Training Center (CMTC) located in Hohenfels, Germany, combat units like the 2nd Dagger Brigade train under realistic wartime conditions. The combined arms warfare is one focus of the various exercise scenarios. The training is a challenge for all ranks, from driver or infantryman up to the leaders, including the staff officers and brigade commanders. The scenarios connect all the different army weapon systems in a three-dimensional battleground. Additionally, realistic material and personal support is included. Four key elements guarantee the success of the training in the CMTC (whose motto is “Train to Win”): 1) Operations Group; 2) Opposing Force; 3) Realistic terrain (Central European woodland); and 4) Control Center. (Walter Böhm)

IFV ODS of 1-26 INF move to contact. All USAEUR combat units train fully equipped for a minimum of 15 months in the CMTC. As a matter of principle, the units are structured as a brigade with two reinforced battalions. This way, there is one battalion with support units in the “Maneuver Box”, while the other battalion leaders can hold a staff exercise in the War Lord simulation center. During this time, the troops train on a platoon or company level. (Walter Böhm)

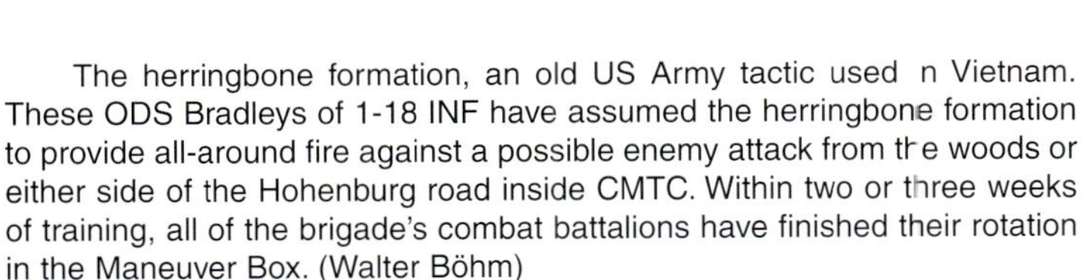

The herringbone formation, an old US Army tactic used in Vietnam. These ODS Bradleys of 1-18 INF have assumed the herringbone formation to provide all-around fire against a possible enemy attack from the woods or either side of the Hohenburg road inside CMTC. Within two or three weeks of training, all of the brigade’s combat battalions have finished their rotation in the Maneuver Box. (Walter Böhm)

To carry the crew’s personal gear, the ODS Bradley is fitted with small eyelets on the sides of the hull. Notice the spare track on the rear of the hull and the lettering “Show me” on this M2A2 ODS IFV Bradley from 1-18 INF. (Walter Böhm)

The 1st Bn, 18th Infantry (nickname "Dogface Battalion") belongs to the 2nd Dagger Brigade. The battalion uses the battle marking number "40" for the battalion. The "42" represents Bravo Company. The Dogface Battalion's history can be traced back to 1861. (Walter Böhm)

This ODS IFV Bradley belongs to the second-in-command of B Company, 1-18 INF. The rear ramp is fitted with an extra oval door for mounting or dismounting when the main ramp is closed. The towing rope is fitted to the ramp beneath the door. Note the three periscopes on the hatch at the rear of the hull. The two fire ports in the ramp remained in the A2 ODS version. (Walter Böhm)

"Blue Spade", an ODS IFV Bradley of C Company, 1-26 INF. Here an infantry squad leaves their battle taxi by way of the hydraulic ramp. With the introduction of the ODS version, the mechanized infantry also now have two Javelin anti-armor missiles and three AT- 4 anti-tank weapons on every ODS Bradley. (Walter Böhm)

During Field Year 2000, the mechanized infantry battalions of 1st US AD and 1st US ID were issued 135 new ODS Bradley vehicles for each division. (Walter Böhm)

"Squad Seating". The six soldiers of an infantry squad are placed three on each side of the rear crew compartment. (Walter Böhm)

The steel side skirts mounted on the hull sides should protect the lower part of the hull, track and carriage against hollow-head rounds. A further modification on the ODS standard is the rubber mounting for extra water canisters, MREs, or baggage on the second front side skirt. (Walter Böhm)

M2A2 ODS IFV Bradley of 1-18 INF. Notice the lettering "Gun Slinger" on the rear of the vehicle. The front hull and turret have been covered with camouflage nets, which is unusual in the CMTC since the MILES II sensors do not work when covered. (Walter Böhm)

This M2A2 ODS IFV Bradley of 1-26 INF slipped in a large mud hole and must be pulled out with the help of an M88A1 recovery tank. (Walter Böhm)

When there is no recovery tank available, the Bradleys must help each other. The ODS drive train, with its 600hp engine and gearbox with three forward and one reverse gear, has enough power to handle emergency recovery situations. (Walter Böhm)

Both M2A2/M3A2 ODS Bradley versions have two means of covering themselves with smoke against hostile observation. First, the two quadruple smoke grenade launchers on the turret and, second, a smoke generator that uses fuel for covering the vehicle with white fog. (Walter Böhm)

If the orange "hit" light of the MILES II gear is flashing continuously, the vehicle has received a deadly hit. Now the crew has to turn their turret to the 6 o`clock position with the gun barrel to the rear, indicating to everyone who sees them that the vehicle is "dead". This M2A2 ODS IFV Bradley was killed by the CMTC OPFOR unit 1-4 INF in Bowling Alley Valley, the nickname of a flat, wide area in the CMTC that is surrounded by hills. The OPFOR unit's performance is one of the key elements of succesful training. (Walter Böhm)

A Bradley team in front of their ODS Bradley. Notice the MILES II webbing on the soldiers and the tank. Introduced in the 1980s, the MILES training system has been continuously improved and made adaptable to newly deployed arms and weapon systems. (Walter Böhm)

During CMTC rotation in May 2001, units of the 2nd Dagger Brigade used an improved version of the MILES II training system. One updated element is shown here fitted to the TOW launcher. (Walter Böhm)

With the improved MILES II, the Army's AH-64A Apache and UH-60 Blackhawk helicopters can now be integrated into the wargaming of the ground forces. (Walter Böhm)

The US Army has fielded 267 Bradley Stinger vehicles, most of them based on the M2A2 version. The vehicles require only minor modifications to transport the two Stinger gunners and their staff in the rear crew compartment. The Stinger Bradley was the replacement for the obsolete M163 20mm self-propelled Vulcan air-defense system based on the M113 carriage. Now the Stinger man-portable ground-to-air missiles and the 25mm Bushmaster gun should protect armored units against hostile air attack. (Peter Siebert)

Shown here is a Bradley Stinger FV of 1st Bn, 4th Air Defense Artillery Regiment, 1st US AD. In addition to the three crewmembers (commander, gunner and driver), there are two Stinger gunners located in the rear of the hull. Also located there are the mounts for two ready-for-use Stingers and four reserve missiles. The Stinger Bradley is considered to be an interim model until the Bradley M6 Linebacker is fielded. (Peter Siebert)

MLRS M270 of 1st Bn, 33rd Field Artillery Regiment, 1st US ID Division Artillery during Exercise “Lion Pride 2000” in the area of Tirschenreuth, Bavaria, Germany. The MLRS chassis uses many components of the Bradley carriage and drive train. The launcher carries twelve missiles on two racks. (Walter Böhm)

An MLRS of the 94th Field Artillery Regiment, 1st US AD Division Artillery pictured during Exercise "Rolling Steel 99". The armored cabin has enough space for the three crewmembers and can protect them against small arms fire and mortar and artillery fragments. (Walter Böhm)

The first MLRS M270s were fielded in 1982, one year after the introduction of the M2/M3 Bradley FV. During the Cold War era, the MLRS gave the USAEUR an effective artillery punch to defeat the Warsaw Pact's "follow-on" forces. Pictured here is an MLRS of 1st Bn, 27th FA, V US Corps Artillery during Exercise "Real Gunners 16/2000" in Bavaria, Germany. (Walter Böhm)

In 1983 the first US Army MLRS artillery battalion showed its reaciness during live fire exercises in Grafenwöhr. Until 1990, the MLRS units based in Germany painted their vehicles in the older US Army MERDC camouflage scheme, like that seen on this vehicle from 40th Field Artillery Regiment, 3rd US AD "Spearhead". The 227mm M26 missiles are packed in seperate pods, each containing six rockets. (Walter Böhm)

In order to replace the aging M577A2 CPV, the US Army started fielding the new M4 Commanc and Control Vehicle (C2V). The M4 is basec on the modified M270 MLRS chassis. The initial production began with a small number of 49 vehicles in fiscal year 1997. The 4th Infantry Division (mech) received five C2Vs for troop trials during the Task Force XXI Program. Tactical exercising to prove this "Army for the 21st Century" program was held in NTC in March 1997. (Peter Siebert)

The REFORGER 92 exercise "Caravan Guard" was the first time the M4 C2V was tested in Germany by the 3rd US ID (mech). The new command vehicle can follow the M1A1 Abrams MBT and the M2/M3 Bradley FV units on the battlefield and continually operate during a road march, too. This is its big advantage over the aging M577A2 CPV. (Peter Siebert)

The greater agility of the M4 C2V in combination with modern electronic systems for communication and control allow the troop commanders to better lead heavy force operations. When using the M4 C2V as a stationary command post, a 10-meter-high antenna can be erected. In the future, two M4 C2Vs will replace four M577A2 CPVs in the armored units. (Peter Siebert)

This XM5 Electronic Fighting Vehicle System Carrier (EFVS) prototype vehicle looks very similar to the M4 C2V. The main difference is the 30-meter-high foldable antenna. The interior of the vehicle is fully packed with systems for electronic warfare. The exact choice of electronic equipment used on board the XM5 is still in progress and is kept secret. The prototype of the EFVS was completed in 1986 and handed over to the Army in 1989. For the REFORGER 90 exercise "Centurion Shield", a vehicle was shipped to Germany to participate in the exercise as part of 1st US AD, 501st Military Intelligence Battalion. This photo shows the XM5 EFVS after the completion of an exercise near the Nördlingen railway station in Bavaria, Germany. (Egon Merk)

"Thunder Lizard", HQ Troop, 1st SQDN, 1st CAV, Grafenwöhr, April 1994. (Walter Böhm)

"982" (Hit Score!), C Troop, 1st SQDN, 1st CAV, Grafenwöhr, April 1994. (Walter Böhm)

"Controlled Chaos – Smith & Wesson", 3CAV5, northern Bosnia, September 1996. (Walter Böhm)

"Our Boopty", 3CAV5, northern Bosnia, September 1996. (Walter Böhm)

"Silencer", B Company, 1-36 INF, CMTC Hohenfels in May 1999. (Walter Böhm)

"Bravo Warriors", B Company, 1-36 INF, CMTC Hohenfels in May 1999. (Walter Böhm)

B Company, 1-36 INF, CMTC Hohenfels in May 1999. (Walter Böhm)

D Company, 2-6 INF, CMTC Hohenfels in May 1997. (Walter Böhm)

B Company, 2-6 INF, CMTC Hohenfels in May 1997. (Walter Böhm)

"Benford's Tool of Destruction", B Company, 2-2 INF, CMTC Hohenfels in June 1999. (Walter Böhm)

"Big Red 1", B Company, 2-2 INF, CMTC Hohenfels in June 1999. (Walter Böhm)

"Destroyers", D Company, 1-36 INF, Friedberg, February 1999. (Walter Böhm)

"Three Stooges", D Company, 4-12 INF, Grafenwöhr, May 1994. (Walter Böhm)

"Renegades", 1-36 INF, CMTC Hohenfels, May 1999. (Walter Böhm)